Microsoft azure

Your personal guide from beginning to pro

Copyright © 2018 by Nate J.

Table of Contents

Introduction

The need for software applications is on the rise. This is coupled with the increase in the number of devices on which software applications can be deployed and used. There are also numerous programming languages that can be used for development of software applications. However, developers usually face a challenge when it comes to getting the infrastructure that is necessary for them to develop and deploy software applications. Sometimes, they lack the tools the necessary for to do the development or acquiring them becomes a challenge. In other times, it is hard to develop applications that scale well, especially with the increase in data and the number of users who need to use the application. Azure is a product from Microsoft that was developed to solve all these problems. It provides developers with a platform where they can develop their applications without having to setup their own infrastructure. It provides the developer with everything that he needs to develop an application. There are a number of programming languages that can be used for development on the Azure platform, including the popular ones like Java, CSharp, and JavaScript etc. This book is a guide for you on how to use the Microsoft Azure platform. Enjoy reading!

Chapter 1- Getting Started with Microsoft Azure

Microsoft Azure provides its users with a Platform as a Service (PaaS) offering. The platform was developed to be used by developers who would like to use it for developing Software as a Service (SaaS) software, databases or services at the backend. The platform has a network of datacenters on which you can develop, deploy and manage services and applications. This means that the platform has a form of operating system, a way of storing data and even more.

The cloud has become a very popular way of storing an accessing data. Users like it because they are provided with a way of storing and accessing the data without using their hard drive. When data is kept in the cloud, it can be accessed from anywhere and at any time. Although the data may keep in a single place in the cloud, it can be synchronized with other web information. A good example of the application of cloud is computing if Office 365. It allows users to create, edit and play around with Microsoft Office documents without having to really install the Microsoft Office product on their computer.
The Azure platform was developed as a way of harnessing the power of the cloud. You can develop a software application or a database on the Azure platform without installing the necessary tools on your computer. For example, you can create a C# application on the Azure platform without being required to install the Microsoft Visual Studio or the SQL database on your computer. This is because the platform comes with these tools. To start using Azure, open **https://portal.azure.com** URL on your web browser. If prompted to sign in, sign in using your Microsoft account, that is, Microsoft email address. You can also use your email address from other email service providers like Gmail, Yahoo etc. You will then be taken to a screen that shows a list of services and applications on the vertical navigation bar located on the left.

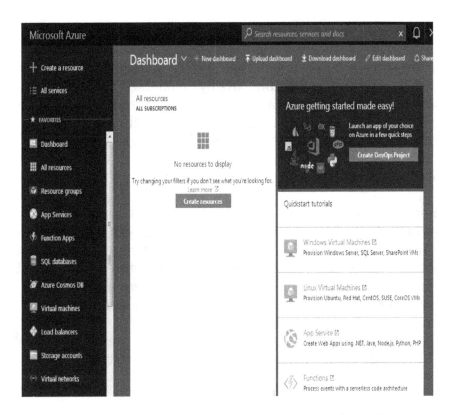

In case you click on any of the categories, you will see its details on the screen.

Chapter 2- Azure Storage

Azure storage is a cloud storage service managed by Microsoft and it provides a durable, highly available, redundant and scalable storage at a cheaper cost compared to when doing the management manually. It comes with different offerings including blobs, tables, queues and file storage.

Storage Accounts

For you to use Azure Storage, you must have a storage account. Once you have created the account, you will be able to transfer data to and from services in the storage account. You are allowed to create a storage account and store up to 500 TB of data. If you are using a Blob storage account and cool or hot access tiers, you can optimize your costs depending on how frequently the data object is accessed.

The storage account can be of the following two types:

- General Purpose
- Blob Storage

General Purpose Storage Account

This account gives us space for storing blobs, files, queues and tables. The services are offered in one account. It can be used for storage of object data, NoSQL data, definition and use of queues for message passing and in setting up file shares in the cloud.

The following are the main storage types in Azure:

- Tables
- Blobs
- Queues
- File Storage

The Azure Table is used for storage of huge amounts of structured data. It is a NoSQL data store accepting authenticated calls from both inside and outside Azure cloud. Azure tables are good for storage of structure, non-relational data.

The Azure Blob is used for storage of unstructured data in the cloud in the form of objects/blobs. It can store any type of binary or text data, like media file, document or an application installer. The Blob storage is also known as object storage.

Azure queue helps in storage of several messages. The messages are accessible from any geographical location via authenticated calls facilitated by HTTPS and HTTP. One queue message may be 64 KB in size and the queue may have millions of messages.

The File Storage share is simply a SMB file share in Azure. All files and directories have to be created in parent share. AN account may have an unlimited number of shares, and the share may store an unlimited number of files, totaling up to 5 TB in size.

We need to demonstrate how to create a website. Files will be uploaded to the blob service. After a file has been uploaded, its details will be added to Azure queue, and this will be used for changing the background of the website once it is refreshed. You should begin by creating a storage account. The following steps can help you do this:

Click "Storage Accounts" on the left pane.
Click on "Add"

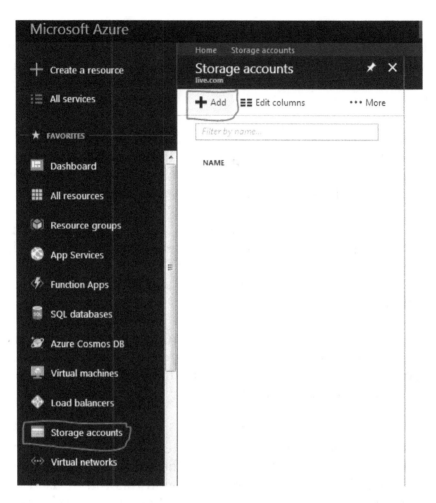

Click "Create Storage Accounts". Enter all the details that are required. Lastly, click "Create".

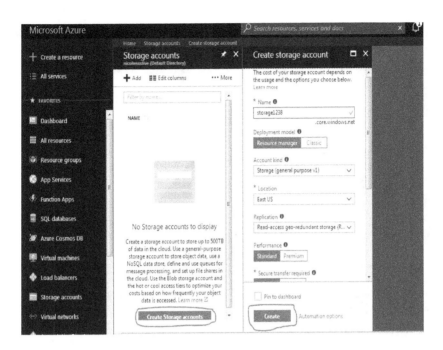

You will then have created a storage account successfully. Our account has four types of storage services namely Blobs, Queues, Files and Tables. We need to demonstrate how to use the Blob and the Queue.

Let us now configure our Blob service. Begin by opening the storage account you have just created. You have to click on the "Storage Accounts" from the left page, and a new window will appear showing the available storage accounts. Click the one you have just created:

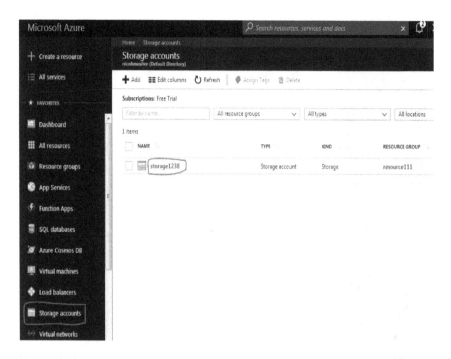

Choose "Blobs" from the window that is opened.

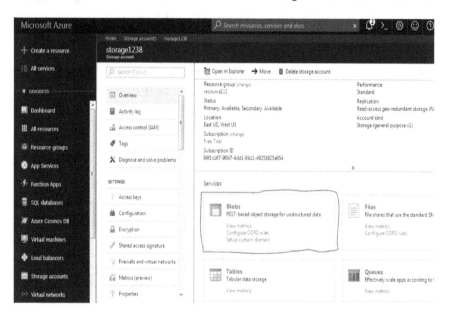

Click "Containers" from the left pane of the pop up, then click "+Container" option so that we may create a new container.

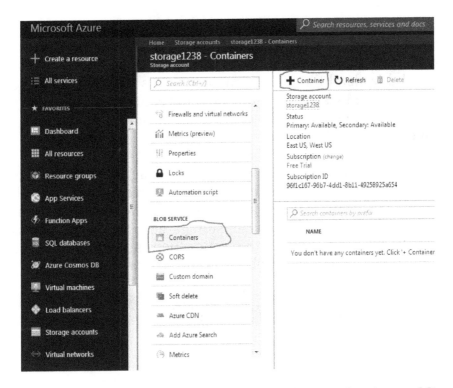

Enter a unique name for the container then assign it a public access level. Blobs are simply files.

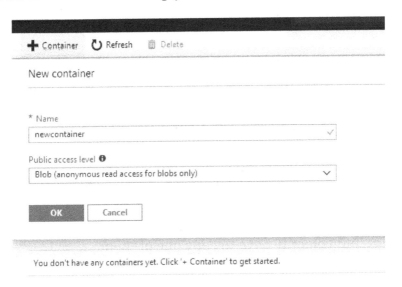

If it is assigned a private access level, then only you will be in a position to download its files. If you assign it a blob access level, then any user with link to the Blob will be able to access it and download files. The container access level gives anyone access to the files and the folders in the container. That is why we have chosen the Blob access level for our container. Once done, click the OK button.

You should now specify a connection string for your storage account in the website code. The connection string will authenticate your code for interaction with the storage account and its services. Choose your storage account, select access keys then copy any of the connection strings. Paste the connection string in the website's code. You will be done!

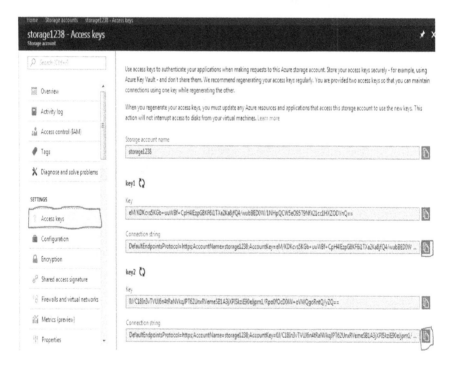

In the above screenshot, I have indicated two connection strings, but you only have to copy one of them.

We now need to begin with the queue. On the popup window for the storage account, ensure you have selected the "Overview" option from the left page, and then choose "Queues".

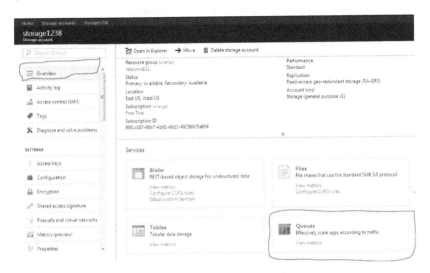

Click the "+ Queue" option so as to create a new queue. Give it a name then click the OK button.

Give the queue a name then click the OK button. You can then substitute the information in your code. You can then go to the website you have created and try to upload a file. You will find that that the file will successfully be added to the container and the queue. You can go ahead and check whether you have an entry in your Blob. You can also open the process page of your website to check whether you can read the entry to the queue and the blob. The name of the image should be similar.

File Service

This service in Azure uses the SMB 3.0 protocol for transfer of files. The service can be attached to the Windows OS as if it is an external drive.

Open the overview page of your storage account, and then choose file service.

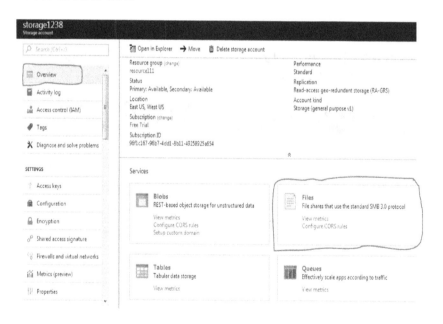

Click the "+ File share" button then give it a name and click the OK button.

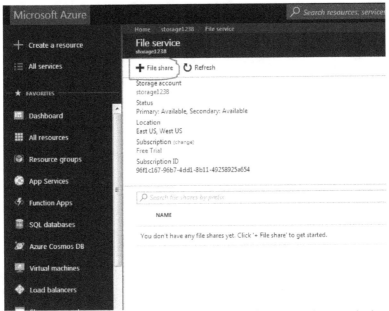

Also, make sure that you have allocated some size to it in the QUOTA section. You can then open the file service that you have created.

Once you have opened the file service, just click the "Connect" button located at the top:

In the new window that appears, just copy the code shown below:

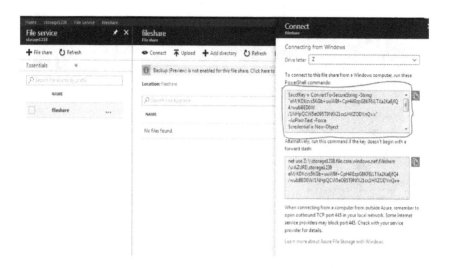

You only need to copy the copy marked with red color above. Paste the code in a text editor like notepad so that you can be able to differentiate its components. The address column should be as follows in the code:

\\storage1238.file.core.windows.net\fileshare

The value for storage1238 and the fileshare should be different in your case based on the name you gave to the storage and the file service.

The username should be as follows:

Azure\storage1238

You will also see the password, which will be close to this:

eM/KDKcvs5KGb+uuWBf+CpH4lEzpG8KF6i1TXa2Ka8jfQ4/wubBED0W/1NHpQCW5eO95T9NfX21cc1HXZODYnQ==

Just save the details as you will need to use them in the next step.

On your computer, identify the "My Computer" or "This PC" icon, right click it then choose "Map network drive". If you are on Windows 7 for example, you should click Start, then right click "My Computer". You will then be able to see the above option which you should see. The following popup will be shown:

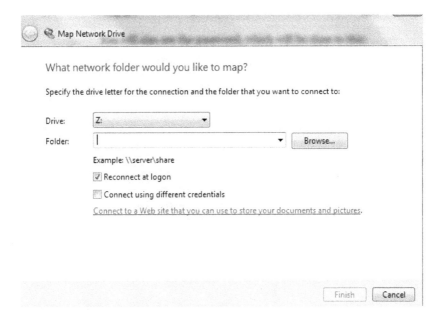

In the field for "Folder", enter the value for column address that you copied from your notepad. This is shown below:

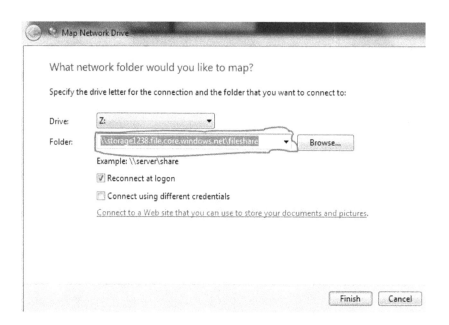

You can then click the "Finish" button to complete this.

A new pop up will appear, just enter the username and the password that you copied from the notepad then click the OK button:

Your drive Azure storage drive is now ready. It is now possible for you to use it for storage on your computer just like any other drive.

Chapter 3- Azure Virtual Network

This provides us with a mechanism of ensuring applications are safe and secure. The virtual networks facilitate communication between various cloud services. It is known as virtual since in the cloud, there are no real routers and switches. If you launch a website server and a database server in the cloud, a medium through which they can interact will be needed. This medium is the one we refer to as the virtual network.

The AVN (Azure Virtual Network) gives you a representation of your network in the cloud. It's just a local isolation of the Azure cloud that is dedicated to your subscription. For two computers to communicate with each other, they should have permissions to do so. Such permissions can be added or removed in virtual network settings. Once the permissions have been added, you can add the computers to the virtual network.

Below are the main components of a virtual network:

- Subnets
- Network Security Groups

In Azure, every virtual network may be divided into sub-parts, which are referred to as subnets. The subnet can further be divided into a private subnet and a public subnet. A private subnet is a network in which there isn't internet access. This is not the case with a public subnet as there is internet access.

Network Security Groups

This provides you with a place to do connection setting configuration like the ports that are to be opened. By default, all ports are closed. To demonstrate this, we will be deploying two servers in the virtual network, a database and a website server. We shall then be able to see how the two can interact with each other.

Let us begin by creating a network security group.

Open the dashboard of your Azure portal then search for network security group. Open it when presented:

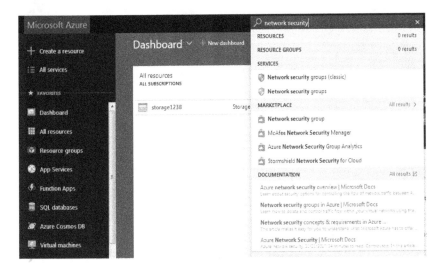

You can as well click the "+ Create New Resource" button located on the left pane, click on "Network" in the new window that appears then choose a "Network security group".

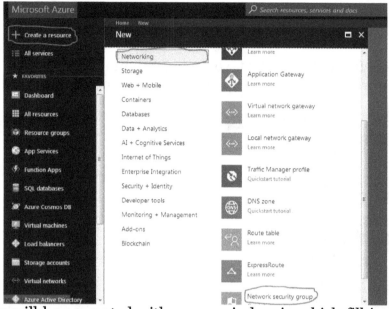

You will be presented with a new window in which fill in the details for the security group. All the resources should be kept in the same group to make it easy to manage them.

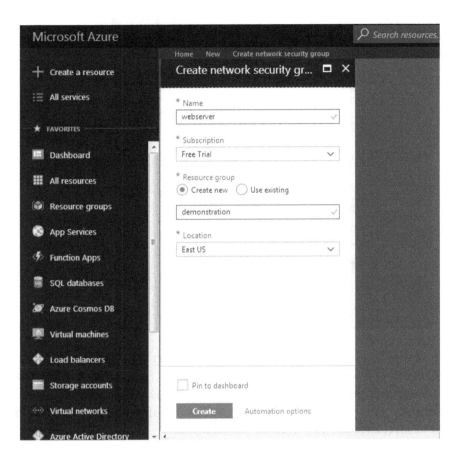

Once you have filled in the necessary details, just click the "Create" button and the network security group will be created.

We can then go ahead to create a virtual network. In the main dashboard of your Azure portal, click the "Virtual networks" from the pane located on the left of the window. In the new screen, click "+ Add" to add a new virtual network.

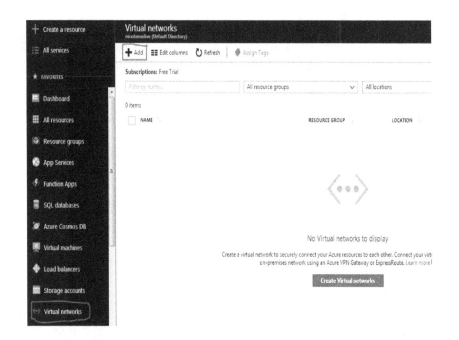

A new window will be presented on which you can add details for the virtual private network. Ensure that in the part for Resource group that you choose "Use existing". You can then choose an existing resource group from the drop down provided below that. This is shown below:

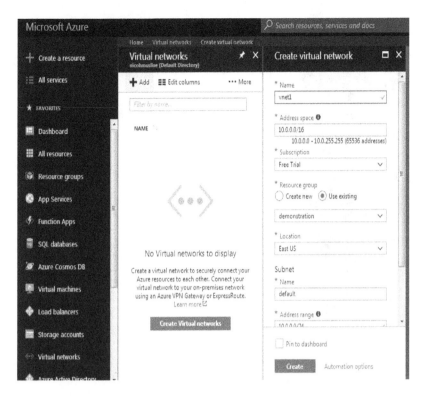

Once done, click the "Create" button and the virtual network will be created.

We can then go ahead and create two subnets. One will be for the website and the other one will be for the database.

Click the "Virtual networks" option from the navigation pane provided in the left side of the screen. In the window that appears, click "Subnets" from the left navigation pane. You can then click the "+ Subnet" button so as to create a new subnet.

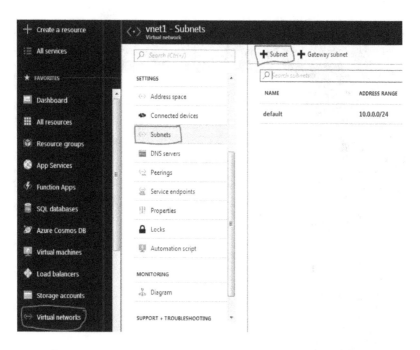

Ensure that you follow similar steps to create two subnets, one for the website and another one for the database.

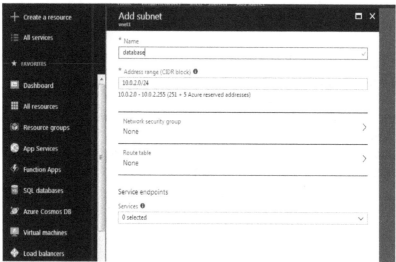

Once you have filled in the details for each subnet, you only have to click the OK button and the subnet will be created.

If the subnets have been created successfully, you will be able to see them in the main window as shown below:

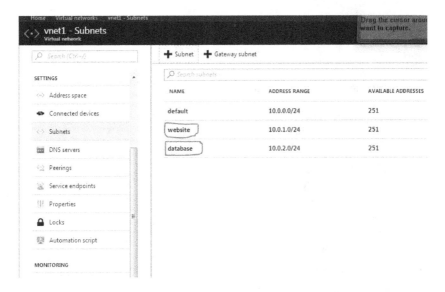

Our network is now set. We only need to go ahead and configure the Network Security Groups then create the servers inside the virtual network. Let us begin by creating the web server:

On the left pane of the main dashboard, click "Virtual machines", then click "+ Add" to create a new one.

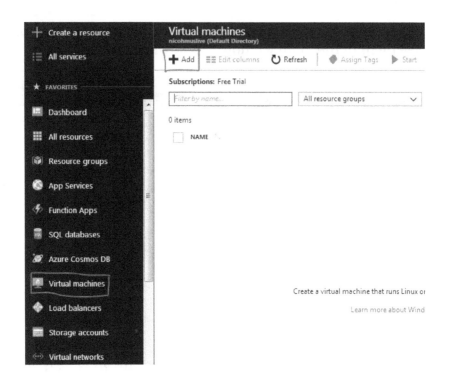

In the window that appears, you will be expected to select an operating system that you need to use. In my case, I will choose the "Ubuntu server" OS for its simplicity, and since this is only for demonstration purposes.

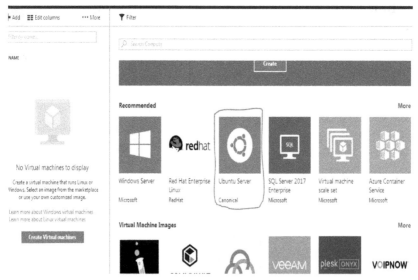

After choosing Ubuntu, just click the "Create" button so as to create it. A new widow will be presented requiring you to enter all the necessary information. For the case of Authentication type, just choose password then enter and confirm the password. For the Resource group, choose to use an existing group then select from the list of groups that you have created. Once you have filled all the details for it, just click the "OK" button:

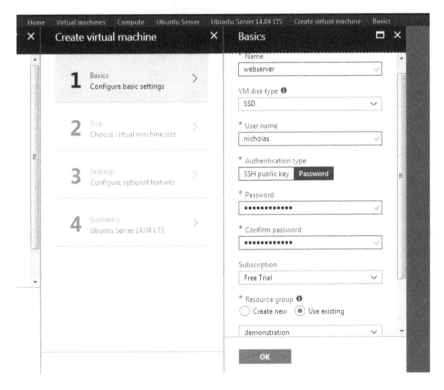

In the next screen you will be required to choose the relevant configuration. We will be using the most basic configuration for demonstration purposes. If the configuration for the basic settings will be successful, a tick will be shown in its section and you will be taken to the page for size. In this page, let us choose the first one which is "Standard". This provides us with the most basic features. After choosing it, click the "Select" button:

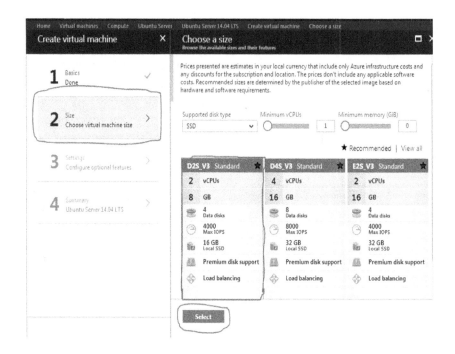

If successful, you will e taken to the next window where you will be required to choose the virtual network in which you need the virtual machine to work. Just choose the virtual network that you had created. Once you click it, it will be shown on the right, and you will also be given an option of creating a new virtual network.

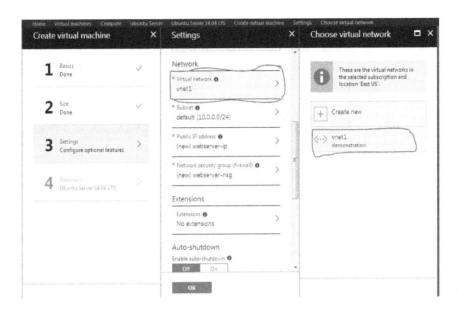

Click the option for "Network security group" and on the right, choose "None". This is because the network security group has already been attached to a virtual network. You can then click the OK button and the deployment of the VM will begin.

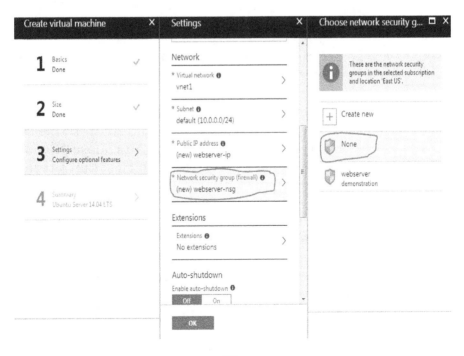

33

You will be taken to the Summary page where you will be required to allow Microsoft to update you regarding the product. Just activate that option and click the Create button:

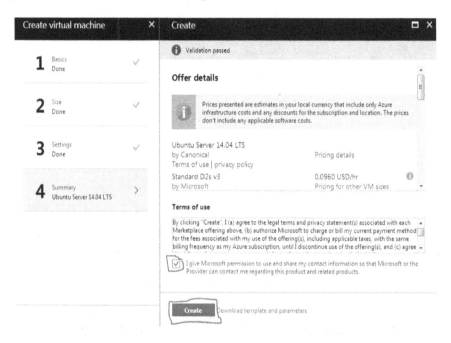

You have successfully created your web server. You should then do the same steps for the DB server.

You have to go to the main dashboard then click on "Virtual machines". Next, you have to click the "+ Add" button so as to create a new virtual machine. Again, you can choose Ubuntu as the operating system to be used, and then click the "Create" button.

Give the virtual machine a name. For the case of authentication, again, choose a password. Don't forget to enter the username. For the case of Resource groups, choose to use an existing resource group then select it from the drop down button. Once you are done, just click the "OK" button and you will be done with the basic configuration.

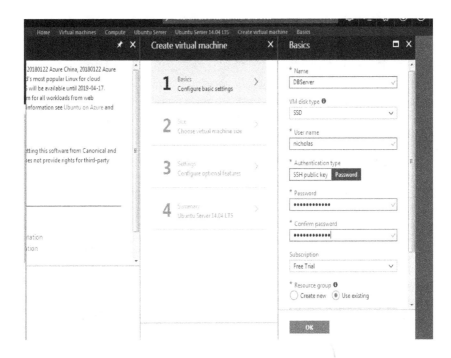

For the case of Size, we will want to use the basic one. Choose the first standard one, and then click the "Select" button. You will be taken to the section for choosing the virtual network that you need to use. Choose the virtual network that you chose when creating the VM for the web server. For the case of the security groups, just choose none has done previously. Once done, click the OK button and you will be done with that part.

You will then be taken to the Summary page. Just activate the option to allow Microsoft update about anything about the product. Once done, click the "Create" button. You will see that the virtual machine for the database server will be created.

Let us now demonstrate something. Open the web server, and then click "Inbound security rules". You can then click the "+ Add" button in the window that appears. Note that you have added nothing to the inbound security rules, so in case I try to use an IP address to connect to a server, I will get an error. This means that for us to be able to add any connection property, we must add an inbound security rule. Let us demonstrate how this can be done:

Open the virtual machine to which you need to add the inbound security rule to. This can be the web server or the dbserver. On the navigation pane on the left of the new window and below SETTINGS, click Inbound security rules. A new window will be opened. You should now click the "+ Add" button at the top of this window.

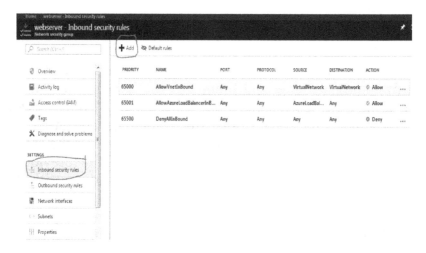

You will get a new window in which you should specify the various details about the inbound security rule.

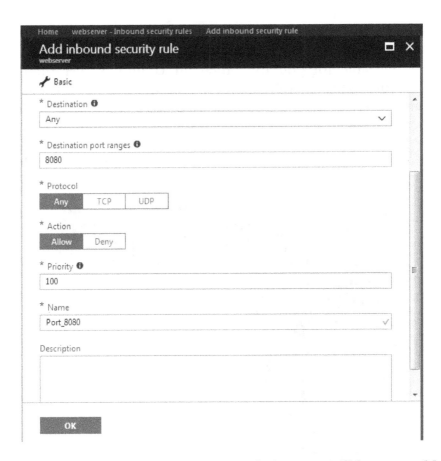

For you to be able to access your website, you will have to add both HTTP and HTTPS connections. SSH will also be needed for server configuration. Just add then try to connect to the server. The response should be okay this time.

Chapter 4- Launching an Ubuntu Server

It is possible for you to launch an Ubuntu server on the Microsoft Azure portal. It is after signing into your account that you will be able to create an Ubuntu virtual machine. Just open **https://portal.azure.com** then log into your account.

On the navigation pane on the left, click the option written "Virtual machines".

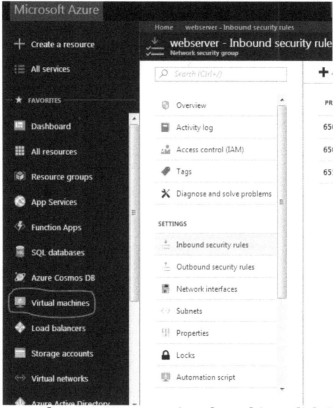

Since we need to create a new virtual machine, click "+ Add" button located at the top.

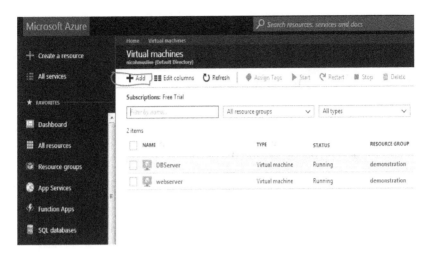

You will then be presented with a new window showing a list of operating systems for which you can create a virtual machine. Since we are creating an Ubuntu virtual machine, choose "Ubuntu". You can then choose the version of Ubuntu that you will need to create a virtual machine for on the window located to the right of the screen. In my case, I have chosen Ubuntu 17.10 as shown below:

You can choose the version that you need based on your requirements. Once done, click the "Create" button located on the right of the screen. You only have to use the scrollbar located on the bottom of the screen and scroll the screen to the right. You will be able to see that button.

You will be taken to a new page on which you specify the details for the virtual machine. You have to give the machine a name, choose the type of disk to be used, choose a username and select the type of authentication that will be used. The username will be used to log into the Ubuntu virtual machine, using the password or the SSH key that you specify to use.

If you need to perform authentication using an SSH key, you must use PuttyGen software to generate the key. The use of a password is the simplest mode of authentication as you are only required to set the password by entering and then confirming it.

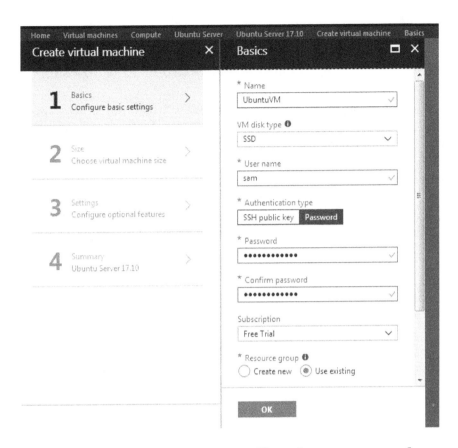

For the case of the resource group, if you have not created one, just choose "Create new" and you will be guided through the process of creating a resource group.

If you have created one, just choose "Use existing" then choose it from the drop down menu provided below that. If you need to perform the authentication using an SSH key, following the steps given below in order to generate the SSH key to be used for this purpose:

1. Open PuttyKeyGen software.
2. Click Generate.
3. Copy the key that is generated from the text box.
4. Click on "save private key" then save the ppk file in a location that you can easily access.

41

Now that you have generated and copied the key, just paste it in the box for SSH public key. Once you have done everything, click the "OK" button and you will be taken to the next step.

In the next screen, you will be required to choose the size of the machine that is to be created. Since we are only demonstrating, it will be good for you to choose the smallest size. Choose the first standard type, then click "Select" so as to select it.

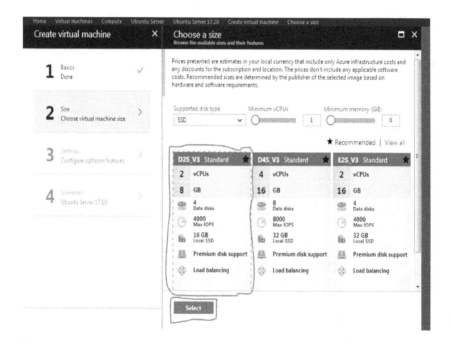

In the next step, you will be asked to configure a number of settings. It is recommended that you don't change any setting, but leave all at their default. Just click the "OK" button to move to the next step:

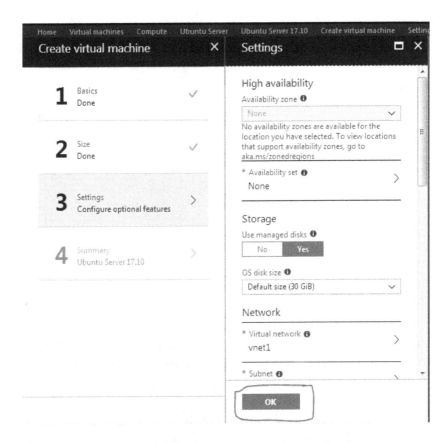

The summary page will ask you to confirm whether you agree with the way the settings have been configured. You only have to click the "Create" button and the virtual machine will be created:

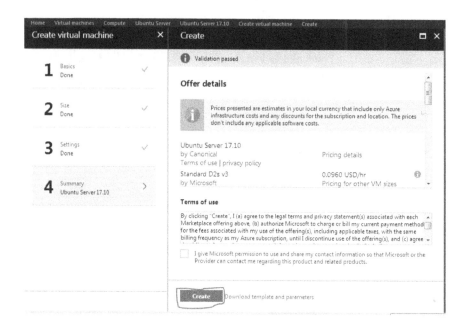

If you need to be getting notifications from Microsoft about the virtual machine that you have created, you should activate the checkbox shown in the page. If the creation of the virtual machine was successful, it will be shown on the dashboard. The submission of the deployment of the virtual machine may take some time based on the speed of your internet. Remain patient and it will complete after some time.

You can click the instance that has been created to see details about it. You can then copy its IP address which is shown below:

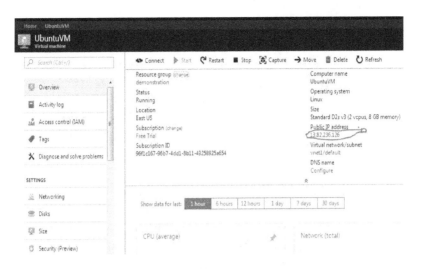

Launch your Putty software. The Putty software can help you establish an SSH connection to the instance that you have created in the cloud. Paste the IP address that you have just copied from the instance into the field for Host name (or IP Address). For the type of connection, choose SSH. The SSH on the left pane will be expanded, just click "Auth".

You will then be asked to provide the private key file for authentication purpose. Just browse to the private file that you saved from the PuttyGen software. After finding it, click "Open". You will then be presented with a command window, asking you to enter a username. Just enter the username that you chose during the configuration of the virtual machine instance. Congratulations, your Ubuntu server is now working on the Microsoft Azure.

If you need to launch any other virtual machine running a different operating system, then you should go through similar steps. The only part you will do it is when choosing the operating system. In this case, we chose Ubuntu, but will have to choose the operating whose virtual machine you need to create.

Chapter 5- SQL Databases in Azure

In Azure, the SQL Databases feature provides structures like JSON, relational data, XML and spatial. The feature provides you with a Database-as-a-platform service through which you can run and scale highly available SQL Server databases in the cloud. With it, you can create an SQL database in the Azure portal.

The creation of an Azure SQL database is done using a set of defined compute and storage resources. The database is normally created within Azure resource group and in Azure SQL Database Logical Server. The following steps will take you through the process of creating an SQL database within the Azure portal:

Begin by login into your Azure portal account then click the "+ Create a resource" portal located at the top left corner of the screen.

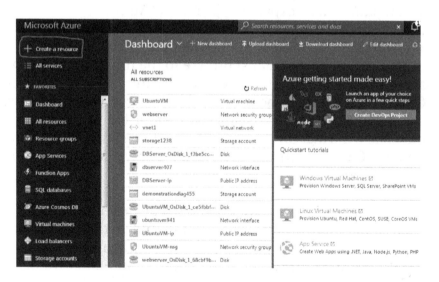

In the new page, choose "Databases" then select "SQL Databases".

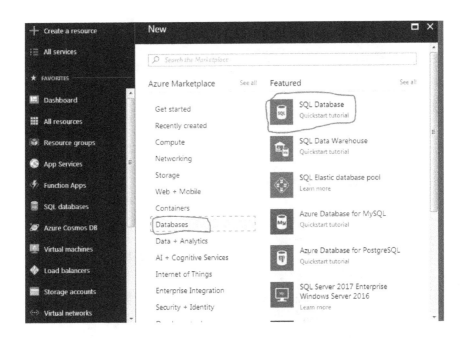

You will then be required to fill in the various details for the database. For the name, give the database a unique name. For the resource group, you can choose to use an existing resource group. For the case of "Select source", you should choose where to get data from for the database. If you need to create a blank database, just choose the appropriate option. If you need to load the database with some data, choose the dataset from which you need to load the data.

The good thing with Azure is that you are provided with some default source from which you can choose to load the data. In my case, I have chosen one as shown below:

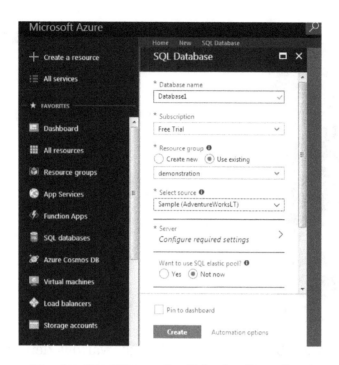

In the section for the "Server", click the "Configure required settings" and you will be prompted to fill in the details for the server. You must provide the details of the server including the server name, the admin username, admin password etc. However, there is a server found, you can select and use it instead of creating a new one.

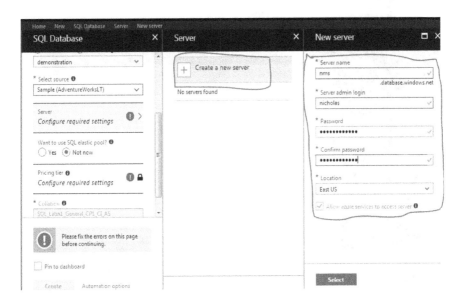

Once you have filled in the details of the server, just click the "Select" button and the server you have just created will be chosen and used for the database.

You can then click the "Pricing tier" so as to choose the pricing tier to be used. This should also help in specifying the number of DTUs as well as the amount of the storage. It is recommended that you explore the options that are available for the storage and DTUs that are available for each service tier. We recommend that you choose the standard tier then by use of the slider, choose 10 DTUs (S0) and storage of 1 GB.

Next, accept preview terms for use of Add-on storage. Now that you have chosen everything, click "Apply" to apply the changes.

Once done with filling all the details for the database, just click the "Create" button. You can also click the notifications icon to see the progress about the deployment of the database. The database will finally be created and deployed. If you click the "SQL Databases" link in the left pane, you will see it as part of the SQL databases that you have created in your portal:

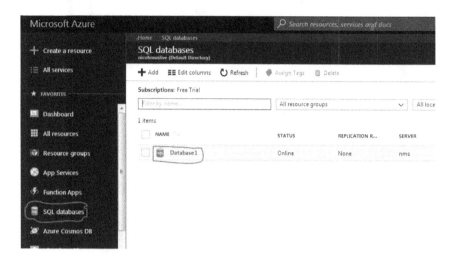

Creating a Firewall Rule

SQL Databases service lets us create a firewall to prevent tools and applications from the external environment from establishing a connecting to the databases running in the server. The firewall is created at server level. even server unless a firewall that opens the firewall for a particular IP address is created.

The SQL Database normally communicates through port 1433. If you try to connect from the corporate network, the outbound traffic on port 1433 may not be accepted by the firewall of your network. In such a case, you will not be able to connect to the Azure SQL Database server before the IT department has opened the port 1433.

The following steps will help you configure an SQL Database server-level firewall route:

Once the deployment of the database has completed, move to the left pane then click the "SQL databases" option, then click the database that you have created. In my case, I had named it "Database1", so I just click that.

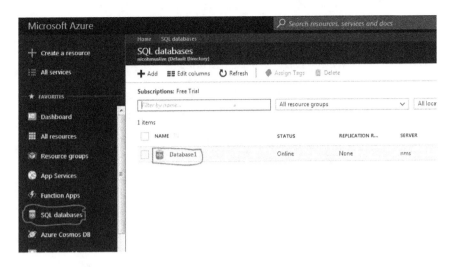

The overview page of your database will be opened showing you all the details of your database. You will also be shown a number of options for a further configuration.

Copy the server name as you will need in the next steps for connection to your server.

On the toolbar located at the top, click the option written "Set server Firewall". You will get a new page with the firewall settings for your SQL Server database.

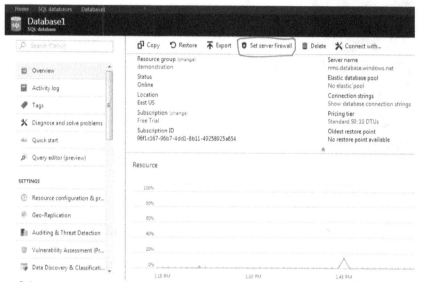

In this new page, click "Add client IP" so as to add the current IP address to the new firewall rule. A firewall rule is capable of opening port 1433 for single IP address or some range of IP addresses.

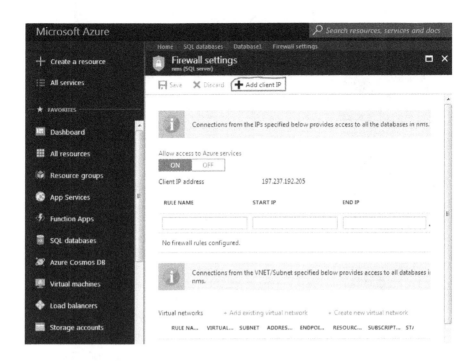

You can then click the "Save" option. You will have created a server-level firewall rule for the current IP address opening the port 1433 on your logical server. The firewall settings will be updated.

Once done, click the "OK" button then close the firewall settings page.

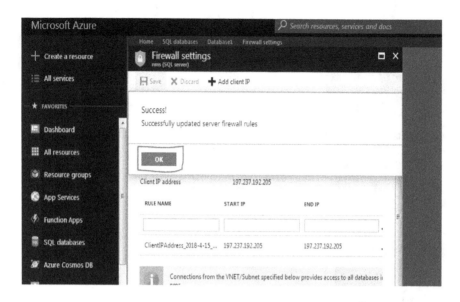

After that, you will be in a position to connect to the SQL Database Server as well as its databases using the SQL Server Management Studio or any other tool that you prefer by use of this IP address and via the server admin account that was created previously. Note that the default setting is that access via SQL Database firewall is allowed for all the Azure services. If you need to disable it for all the Azure services, just click the OFF option and it will be disabled.

Querying the Database

Our database has been created and populated with some data. We can now try to query it so that we can see whether we can connect to it. We will use the built-in query tool. Follow the steps given below:

On the page with the details about your database, click the option for "Query editor (preview) on the left pane. Alternatively, you can reach this by clicking the "SQL Databases" option from the main dashboard then clicking the name of your database.

You can then click on "Login".

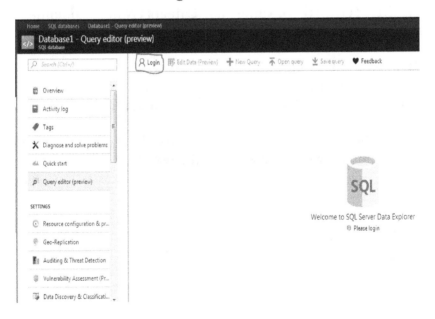

We need to use SQL server authentication to login, so choose this option and provide the necessary login information to your SQL Server. Once done, click the OK button.

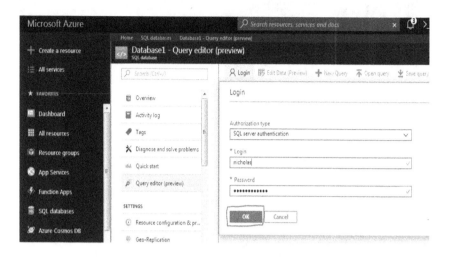

The query editor pane will be opened on which you can run your SQL queries. You can type the following sample query on the query editor:

SELECT TOP 10 p.Name as CategoryName, p.name as ProductName

FROM SalesLT.ProductCategory p
JOIN SalesLT.Product pp
ON p.productcategoryid = pp.productcategoryid;

To run the query and see the results, just click the "Run" button and you will be able to see the results.

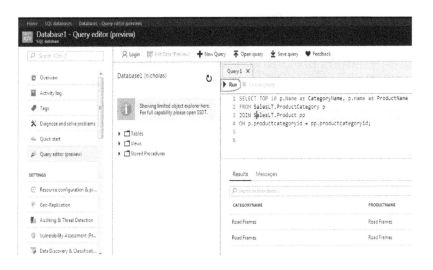

That is how you can query the database. The results are shown at the bottom of the query window as shown above. You can now close the query window and any unsaved edits will be discarded.

Chapter 6- Azure Functions

Azure functions provide you with a way of running some small pieces of code commonly known as functions. You are allowed to write and run a function without having to worry about the infrastructure on which you will run it. With functions, development becomes easy and you are allowed to select a language of your choice like C#, F#, Java, Node.js, or PHP. The Azure is capable of scaling according to the needs of your functions.

Creating a Function App

For you to be able to execute functions in Azure, you should first create a function app that will help in hosting this. The following steps can help you create a function app in Azure:

Begin by login into your Azure portal account, then click the " + Create a resource" button located at the top left of the screen.

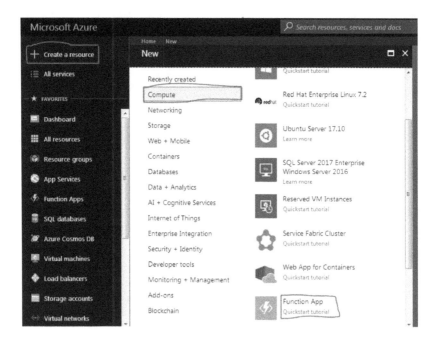

You will be presented with a new window on which you should specify the settings for your function app. You can specify the settings as shown below:

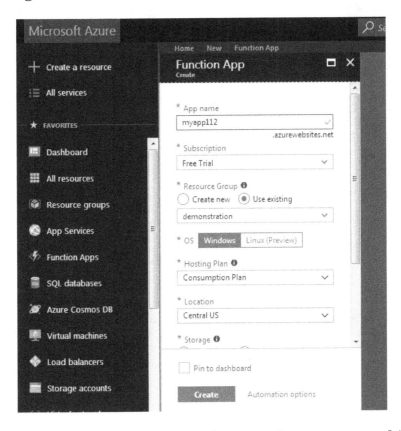

You must give the app a name. The operating system on which the app will run should also be chosen, which in my case I have chosen Windows. You must also specify a resource group for the function app, which can be an already existing resource group or create a new one. Once done with filling the various settings, just click the "Create" button.

You can click the notifications icon and see the deployment of the app being done. Once completed, you will see a success message.

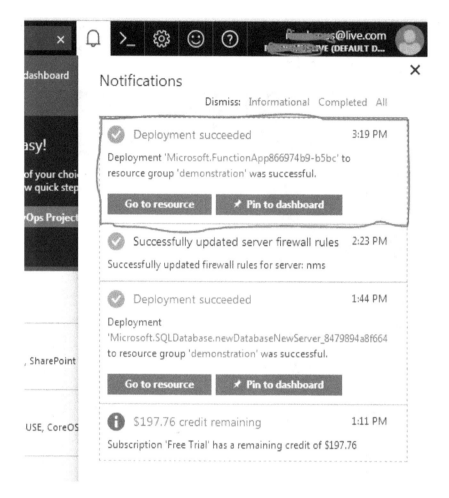

You can then click the button "Go to resource" so as to see the newly created application.

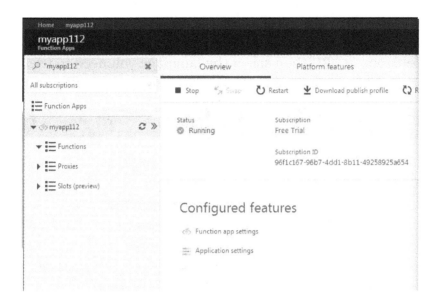

Now that we have created the function app, we can create a function to run within it.

Creating a Function

Begin by expanding the function app that you have created. Click to the "Functions" option and you will see a + button. Click it.

You will get a new page for Get started quickly, choose "WebHook + API" then select the language you need to use for the function. Click on "Create this function".

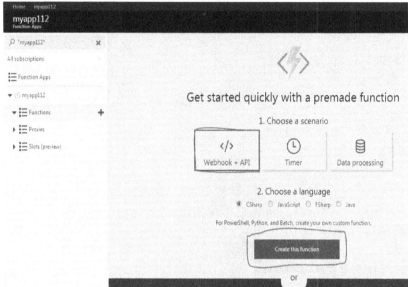

The function will be created for the language that you have chosen. In the above case, I have chosen Csharp, so a Csharp function will be created using the template for HTTP triggered function. The following code is generated automatically:

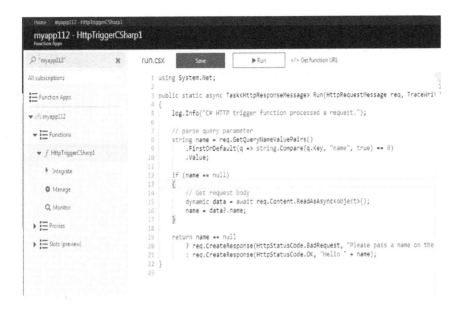

It is now possible for you to run the new function simply by sending HTTP request.

We can now test to see whether the function is working or not. On the window for the function, click the option for "</> Get function URL" located at the top right of the screen.

```
run.csx        Save              ▶ Run      </> Get function URL
1  using System.Net;
2
3  public static async Task<HttpResponseMessage> Run(HttpRequestMessage req, TraceWrit
4  {
5      log.Info("C# HTTP trigger function processed a request.");
6
7      // parse query parameter
8      string name = req.GetQueryNameValuePairs()
9          .FirstOrDefault(q => string.Compare(q.Key, "name", true) == 0)
10         .Value;
11
12     if (name == null)
13     {
14         // Get request body
15         dynamic data = await req.Content.ReadAsAsync<object>();
16         name = data?.name;
17     }
18
19     return name == null
20         ? req.CreateResponse(HttpStatusCode.BadRequest, "Please pass a name on the
21         : req.CreateResponse(HttpStatusCode.OK, "Hello " + name);
22 }
23
```

Choose "default (Function key)" then click "Copy".

63

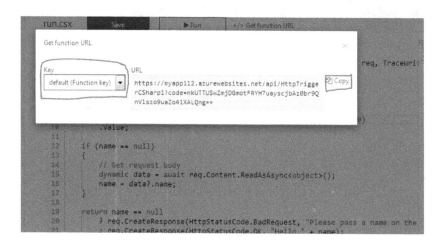

Paste the URL that you have just copied into the URL bar of your web browser. Also, add the following to the end of the URL string then click the Enter key:

&name=<yourname>

In my case, I end with following URL after adding the username to the URL string:

https://myapp112.azurewebsites.net/api/HttpTrigger CSharp1?code=nkUTTUSwZmjDGmotFRYH7uayscjb Azobr9QnVlszo9uaZo41XALQng==&name=nicholas

After running the function, the trace information is send to the logs. If you need to see the trace information from the previous execution, just return to the function in the portal then click the arrow at the bottom of the screen so as to expand logs. This is shown below:

run.csx [Save] [▶ Run] [</> Get function URL]

```csharp
1  using System.Net;
2
3  public static async Task<HttpResponseMessage> Run(HttpRequestMessage req, TraceWrit
4  {
5      log.Info("C# HTTP trigger function processed a request.");
6
7      // parse query parameter
8      string name = req.GetQueryNameValuePairs()
9          .FirstOrDefault(q => string.Compare(q.Key, "name", true) == 0)
10         .Value;
```

Logs ⌄ | Errors and warnings ⌃   ▌▌Pause 📋Clear 📋Copy logs ⤢Expand

```
2018-04-15T12:40:30  Welcome, you are now connected to log-streaming service.
2018-04-15T12:41:30  No new trace in the past 1 min(s).
2018-04-15T12:42:30  No new trace in the past 2 min(s).
2018-04-15T12:43:30  No new trace in the past 3 min(s).
2018-04-15T12:44:30  No new trace in the past 4 min(s).
2018-04-15T12:45:30  No new trace in the past 5 min(s).
2018-04-15T12:46:30  No new trace in the past 6 min(s).
2018-04-15T12:47:30  No new trace in the past 7 min(s).
2018-04-15T12:48:30  No new trace in the past 8 min(s).
2018-04-15T12:49:22.750 [Info] Function started (Id=5e0b00d2-7fce-492b-b065-7b92165724c9)
2018-04-15T12:49:22.843 [Info] C# HTTP trigger function processed a request.
2018-04-15T12:49:22.843 [Info] Function completed (Success, Id=5e0b00d2-7fce-492b-b065-7b92165724c9, Duration=92
2018-04-15T12:50:02.107 [Info] Function started (Id=274acfc5-d148-4bc6-95be-2d40c3fc0502)
```

Chapter 7- Azure Cosmos DB

This is a feature in Azure that provides us with an easy way of storing JSON and unstructured data. When Cosmos DB is combined with Azure functions, the storage of data is made much easier and quicker using less code compared to what is required when storing data in a relational database.

When using Azure functions, the input and output bindings are a great way of connecting to external service data from the function. Let us discuss how to use an output binding and a Csharp function for storing unstructured data in a Cosmos DB document. We will be using the Csharp function that we had created earlier.

Creating Output Binding

The following steps will help you add an output binding:

Open the page for the function app you had created, and then expand both the function app and the function itself.

Click "Integrate" below the Function, then click "+ New Output" located at the top right of the screen. Select the "Azure Cosmos DB".

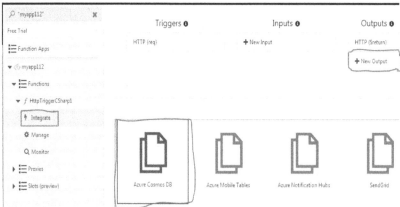

You can then click the "Select" button.

The settings page for the Azure Cosmos DB output will be presented to you, where you should the various settings regarding the same. Just click the "New" option which is located next the "Azure Cosmos DB account connection".

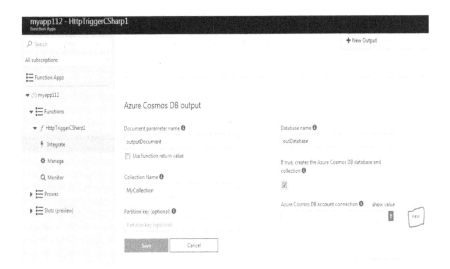

In the next window, choose "+ Create new". A pop up for New Account will be shown. You can enter the following settings to it:

The ID should be the name of the database. This is the Azure Cosmos DB Database, and the name should be unique. For the case of the API, choose SQL. This is because the trigger and outbound bindings in Azure Cosmos DB work with Graph API and SQL API only. For the resource group, use an existing resource group or choose to create one if you don't have one.

You can then click the OK button to create the database. The creation of the database may take a number of minutes, so remain patient. Once the database has been created, the connection string will be kept in the form a function app setting. The name for this will be inserted as the "Azure Cosmos DB account connection".

Once the connection string has been set, just click "Save" to create the binding.

You will have created the binding successfully.

We can now go ahead and update the code for our function. Just replace the current function code with the one given below:

```
using System.Net;

public static HttpResponseMessage Run(HttpRequestMessage
req, out object outputDocument, TraceWriter log)
{
    string name = req.GetQueryNameValuePairs()
        .FirstOrDefault(q => string.Compare(q.Key, "name", true)
== 0)

        .Value;

    string task = req.GetQueryNameValuePairs()
        .FirstOrDefault(q => string.Compare(q.Key, "task", true)
== 0)

        .Value;

    string duedate = req.GetQueryNameValuePairs()
        .FirstOrDefault(q => string.Compare(q.Key, "duedate",
true) == 0)

        .Value;

    outputDocument = new {
        name = name,
        duedate = duedate.ToString(),
        task = task
    };

    if (name != "" && task != "") {
```

```
        return req.CreateResponse(HttpStatusCode.OK);
    }
    else {
        return req.CreateResponse(HttpStatusCode.BadRequest);
    }
}
```

The code will read the HTTP Request query strings then assign them to fields in in outputDocument object. The outputDocument binding will send the object data from the binding parameter which will be stored in bound document database. The creation of the database is done when the function runs for the first time.

Testing the Function and the Database

The following steps will help you test whether what you have created is working: expand the window on the right then choose "Test". Below Query, click "+ Add parameter" then add the parameters given below to your query string.

- name
- task
- duedate

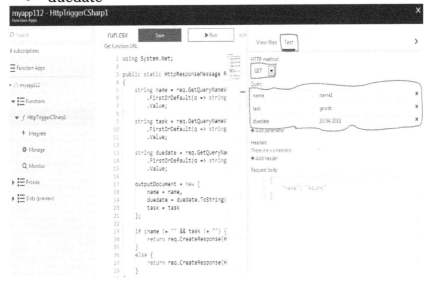

Click the Run button to see the status that you get.

Expand the icon bar located on the left of Azure portal, click inside the search field then type "cosmos". Choose "Azure Cosmos DB" when presented to you as an option.

Select your Azure Cosmos DB Account, and then choose "Data Explorer". Expand the odes for "Collections", then choose the new document, then confirm whether the document has query string values together with additional metadata.

Congratulations. The addition of a binding to HTTP is trigger that is responsible for storing unstructured data in Azure Cosmos DB.

Chapter 8- Adding Messages to Azure Storage Queues

We discussed the use of output and input bindings in Azure. In this chapter, we will be using an output binding for creation of a message in a queue once a function has been triggered via an HTTP request. We will be using the Azure Storage Explorer for viewing the queue messages that have been created by the function. However, you are required to install this tool for you to be able to use it.

Adding Output Binding

We will be using the user interface of the Azure portal to add a binding for the queue storage output to the function that we had created earlier on. This binding makes it possible for us to write a minimal code for creation of a message in the queue. You are not required to write code for some tasks such as opening of a storage connection, creation of a queue and getting a reference to the queue. The Azure queue output binding and Azure Functions runtime will perform such functions on your behalf.

Follow the steps given below:

Login to your Azure portal then open the home page of the function app that you created earlier on. You only have to choose "All Services", and then choose "Function Apps". You can then select your function app, which is the app that you had created.

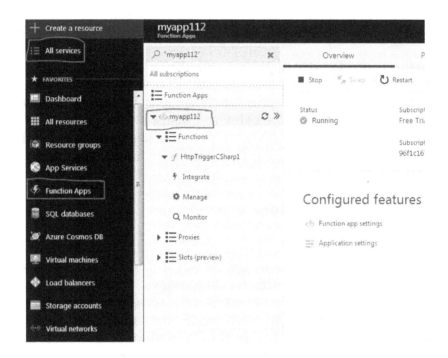

You can then choose Integrate > New output > Azure Queue storage.

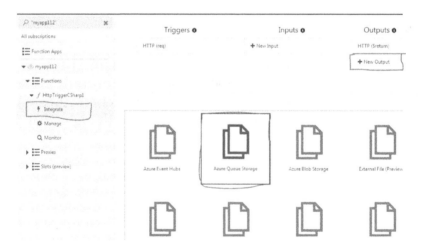

After choosing all the above, just click the "Select" button. You will see a new window with the title "Azure Queue Storage output". Here, you are expected to set settings as shown below. Once done, just click the "Save" button:

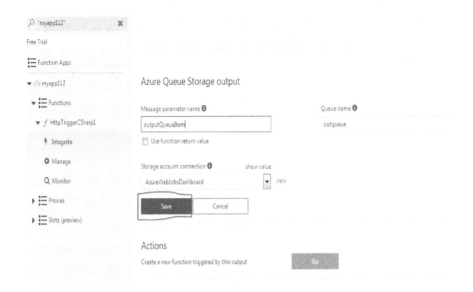

The binding will be added once you have clicked the "Save" button. Now that you have defined an output binding, the code should be updated to use the binding for adding the message to the queue.

Adding a Code that uses Output Binding

We will create code for adding message to output queue. The message should have the HTTP trigger trigger passed to the query string. Example, in case the query has string has "name=Azure", then the queue message will be the Name passed to function: Azure.

Begin by selecting the function to show its code in the editor.

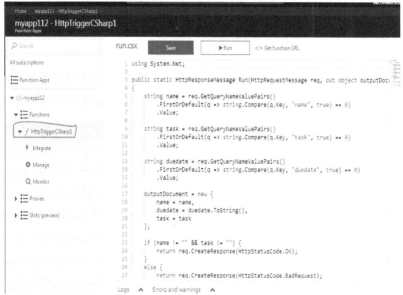

If it is a C# function, then add some method parameter for your binding then write code that will use it. You should also add an outputQueueItem parameter to your method signature as demonstrated below. The name of the parameter should be similar to what you entered for the "Message parameter name" during the creation of the binding. Here is the code:

```
public static async Task<HttpResponseMessage>
Run(HttpRequestMessage req,
    ICollector<string> outputQueueItem, TraceWriter log)
{
    ...
}
```

In the body of your C# function and before "return" statement, add a code to use the parameter for creation of a queue message. This should be as follows:

```
outputQueueItem.Add("Name that was passed to the function: " + name);
```

If it is a JavaScript function, you should add code that uses the output binding on the object named "context.bindings" for creation of the queue message. This is the code that you should add before the "context.done" statement:

context.bindings.outputQueueItem = "Name that was passed to the function: " + (req.query.name || req.body.name);

Once you have made the changes, click the "Save" button to save them.

Now that you have made changes to your function, you need to test it and be sure that it is running correctly. You only have to click the "Run" button and the code will be executed.

The Request body will have the name value of Azure. The value will appear in the queue message that is created after invoking of the function. Other than clicking the "Run" button, the function can also be invoked by entering its URL in a browser and specifying the value of name in a query string. You need to check the logs and ensure that the function has run successfully. After that, a new queue named outqueue will be created in your storage account by functions runtime after using the output binding for the first time. You confirm whether the queue and the message in.

Conclusion

This marks the end of this guide. Microsoft Azure is a cloud computing platform developed by Microsoft. The platform provides you with a platform where you can develop your own applications. When developing applications on Microsoft Azure, your task is only to create the apps without worrying about the infrastructure to use for that purpose. This is because platform has everything that you need to develop and deploy your application. With Azure, you are allowed to develop different applications using different programming languages. These programming languages are the common and popular bones including CSharp, JavaScript, and Java etc. These are the programming languages that are used for development of majority of computer applications with a high demand in the market. This shows how useful the Azure platform is to the developers. They can develop applications using any of the above programming languages without having to setup a programming language in the same way it is done under normal circumstances.

When developing your applications on Azure, you can integrate them with various types of databases. For instance, Azure has the SQL database that you can link to your applications when creating the backend of the application.
Other than that, Azure makes it possible and easy for you to store unstructured data. This is made possible by use of the Azure Cosmos DB which is easy for you to use at any time. After creating a database, you can surround it with a firewall that will determine how your data is accessed. The filtering of connections can be done using the IP addresses of various machines. Unless the IP address of a machine is allowed on the firewall, it won't be able to access the data kept in the database. However, once the IP address of the machine has been permitted, then it will be able to freely access the data stored in the database at any time.

www.ingramcontent.com/pod-product-compliance
Lightning Source LLC
Chambersburg PA
CBHW070854070326
40690CB00009B/1843